MW01487906

Spiritual Indictment

THERE I WAS BUT HERE I AM

To my cuz, Ashley
Keep doing what you do.
And Greater is Coming!!!

JAMES HAWKINS

Copyright © 2018 James Hawkins

All rights reserved.

ISBN: 9781728868844

Imprint: Independently published

DEDICATION

After 15 years of procrastination and self-doubt, the time has come to bring this book to life. As you read through the upcoming pages, my prayer is that you will be empowered and encouraged regardless of your present state. The title of this book There I was But here I Am came from my youth to the present day.

You will experience what life was like through the lens of my eyes and walk through some joyful places and dark places of my life. To expose parts of your life can be very challenging and place you in a position of vulnerability and doubt. I trust that this book will cause you to search yourself and bring your visions to life.

Over the years many have impacted my life that I can't possibly name all of you but know you are loved and appreciated.

However, I have to give special thanks for the support of my wife Dr. Angela Hawkins for the encouragement and support and allowing me to be transparent with the world to write this book from a place before she was my wife. I truly appreciate you more than you will ever know. Thanks for believing I could do this.

Thanks to my Pastor Bishop C. Shawn Tyson and First Lady Evangelist Krista Tyson for your kind words of encouragement and for the opportunity to lead some of the greatest saints in the world at Christ Church Apostolic. I love you all to life, and I must thank the entire CCA family for loving and embracing me and loving me when I moved to Indianapolis.

To my JHM Radio staff, all of you are family to me, and I genuinely appreciate the kind words that have kept me going forward with this project.

Special thank you to Timia Carruthers for your support because when I thought this project was delayed, you wouldn't allow it to die and introduced me to the best Literary Midwife any writer could ask for the one and only Mrs. Nakialah Majors. Thank you for pushing me to write and bring this book to life. To Mr. Warren L. Williams III thank you for all that you do to keep my schedule together and your support in making this project come to life, I appreciate the friend and brother you have become. To my parents, Bishop Ernest and Delores Hawkins for always being prayerful and pushing me to always to keep God first and great things will come forth. Thank you to my Mother Earlene Jones for giving birth to me and loving me regardless of anything or crazy decisions I made over the years and Michael Jones for believing in family and how important it is for family to stay together. To my pride and joy and forever my baby girl Alexis Hawkins I love you.

To my three sons:

James A. Hawkins, Channing Hawkins, Norman Smith. I love you three and thank you for inspiring me to be and do more in life.

Also, finally to my Godmother Kaye Rapier, thank you for your continued support.

Mentors

Bishop J. Lavernge Tyson

Bishop Paul A. Bowers

Bishop Jerry L. Maynard

Dr. Patricia McKinstry

Bishop Leroy Coleman

Mr. Jesse L. Johnson

Thanks to all of my Pastoral Colleagues for giving me the opportunity to minister in your churches. Greater is Coming.

Blessings

ACKNOWLEDGMENTS

Photo Haley Rose Photography

Make-up artist Tamera Payton

Hair Master Barber Rick Woodson

Graphics Chalandon Walker

Assistant Warren L Williams III

Literary Midwife/Publishing Nakilah Majors

JAMES HAWKINS

FOREWORD

My eyes have been opened to the silent cry to the pain of young children, of the pain that has been put upon them by hurting adults. These children grew up to be hurting adults who unfortunately hurt others because of the pain they live with and in. These children left unreached for healing become walking testimonies of the adults that handled them. When you read you will hear the cry of many for James Hawkins. Allow this pain and the victory to become a part of your prayer for children everywhere. Let's not be quick to criticize before we give a helping hand.

First Lady Krista Tyson

JAMES HAWKINS

INTRODUCTION

Wow after many years of trying not to write this book, the time has finally come. It's amazing to me how people think they know you, but they genuinely don't have a clue as to where you come from. We spend so much time seeking approval that we forget about our purpose and in most cases, we lose sight of our destiny, and we never get to that place of fulfillment that was always in our view. However, something other than the devil kept getting in the way of you getting there. It was you that stopped you. We have all heard the saying, "Sometimes we are our worst enemy." Well, I found out in the most challenging ways, because I caused myself a lot of hardships and problems.

Writing this book is so much easier for me now than it was ten years ago. I was just too afraid to tell my story for fear of how people would see or feel about me. I felt like the doors that I needed to have opened for me would never happen if I was transparent. I just knew that the ministry God had given me would be over and nobody would want to hear anything I had to say. Most of all I was afraid of the shame that I would cause my Family.

The good news is I had to get over all of that and be obedient to God, and now I've answered the call, and it feels nothing short of amazing. So, I'm inviting you to take this journey with me as I take you through some of the best and worst and of times I've ever faced in life and how when God does a great work in your life don't be surprised to experience Spiritual Indictment.

I NEVER SAW IT COMING

"The steps of a man are established by the Lord when
he delights in his way. "
Psalms 37:23, ESV

I trust that as you read this book, you will be able to see the transparency that I will convey as it relates to some of my most problematic experiences in life. I was born in small-town Columbia TN in 1967, and my parents were very young at the time. Back then, a woman who was "with child" at the age of 16 had a hard way to go. My mother was looked upon like the woman that had an issue of blood, but my father was not looked upon so harshly because he was the man. Funny how we can judge people and not realize it's at the point where their life is changing forever, all because of a lack of support and the love we should all show toward one another.

I had the good fortune, along with my sister, of being raised in the church. I knew from a very early age what church was like mainly because growing up in the Hawkins home there were no options, you were going to church like it or not. It wasn't like it is today where parents ask their children if they are going to church, it was already understood we were going. I don't get this new age way of thinking where we give our children options, and we wonder why they do some of the things they do. Being raised in the church, I strayed away myself, so I can only imagine the intensity of the fight that most of our young people face today. However, that's not the emphasis of what I want to talk to you about, but it was just a fact that I needed to put out there for what's to come as you read this chapter.

At the age of 12 years old I was going to go through one of the most challenging times of my entire life, my parents deciding to call it quits as it related to their marriage. I knew at times they didn't get along, but such is life I didn't think anyone got along all the time. I know my sister and I didn't always see eye to eye, but at the end of the day we loved each other and would go to war for each other. Now I know I am not the first child to go through his parents becoming divorced from each other, but the way it affected my life is an experience I will never forget.

It changed my life. I remember it like it was yesterday how it all started. My sister and I had a normal life, we went to the best schools, wore the best clothes and lived in one of the best neighborhoods in the city. One morning my mother was gone to work, and my father saw my sister and me off to school as he usually did when he wasn't working. That day I left home I had no idea that when I came home from school that my life would change. So, you could imagine my devastation when my sister and I came back from school one day, and my father was gone. We came home, and all three cars were in the driveway, I went into the house and called my father, "No answer." His

fishing poles were gone, so I assumed he had gone

fishing. As my sister and I looked through the house,

and we realized that wasn't the case. I opened the

closet, and all his clothes were gone, and then it hit me,

this would be the day that would change the entire

course of my life. My dad was gone, and I didn't know

where to find him. At 12 it's a natural reaction to want

to know where your father is and not to know was

torture for me daily. I started to change for the worse

when this life event of my father leaving took place.

Unfortunately, he was gone, and I don't

understand why. I left home and rode my bike for miles

and miles, even to the point of going to all the places

my father and I would go together from stores to family

members homes, and I couldn't find my father. I even

rode my bike to my grandparents' house, and this was about a 6-mile ride.

My father was the man that I went or tried to go everywhere with, if he left the house, trust me when I tell you I was trying to go also. I began to call my dad's friends, no one had seen him, or at least that's what I was told. Now you must understand, my dad was my hero, he took me hunting and fishing. We did so much together, and wherever he went, whatever he did, I wanted to do. My dad was my hero, and now my hero was gone. Now the only man I looked up to and admired was gone, and it would be almost an entire year before I would be reunited with him. As I had to come to terms that my parents were getting divorced life changed for me in a way that I never saw coming.

Now at the age of 12, I had to go from being a boy in the home to what I will refer to as The Protector.

When my father left and moved out of state, he left everything behind, the cars, the house, everything. The one thing I was grateful for was how both of my parents made sure we had the best of the best from as far back as I can remember, but without my father being in the home I decided to become Protector, meaning I'm now the man of the house. To a certain point, my mother allowed me to take on this role, but trust me she only let me go so far. I must admit I took my new-found position in the home serious and went overboard at times. One of the hardest parts of my father being gone was watching my mother struggle to pay bills and take care of my sister and me. I give my mother a lot of credit, she never gave up on us and never had men running in and out of our home. Honestly, I wasn't going to have that anyway. Life was hard enough without my parents being together, so no way was another man about to try and fill that space, because in my heart I sincerely wanted to see my parents come back together, but that never happened. Trust me it wasn't because I didn't try all sorts of tactics to get them together, but I had to come to terms that it was over.

About a year after my parents divorced my mother decided to move to another part of Tennessee (Nashville), my dad had moved to Youngstown, Ohio. I wanted to go live with my dad; however, my mother wasn't having that. She didn't understand why I would want to go live with my dad after he had left. There are always three sides to a story, each person has their perspective to the story and then the truth. Both of my parents have their story as to why my father left and the chain of events that followed. I eventually, had to accept both stories and move on with my life. I loved my parents, and as any child of separation, I hoped that my parents would get back together.

At the age of 13 I desperately wanted to be where my father was in Ohio, and after many times of pleading and begging, my mother decided to allow me to go and live with my Father. I realize it had to be hard for her to let her child go but I felt that my place was with my dad. After all, it wasn't like I wouldn't see my mom and sister during the year and I love my mom and sister, but I knew at 13 my life was headed in a different direction. This place in life, God would be the only one to bring me out.

It was 1980, and my mother allows me to go live with my father in Ohio. I was so happy I didn't know what to do. It was probably a good idea that I left because I wasn't going to let my mother find happiness with another man, while I was around. I was a proverbial "mess." I would pride myself on being disrespectful and unruly whenever my mother had male company. I was determined not to let any man besides my father date my mother. My mother knew I needed guidance, she knew I was hurting and needed my father, so she agreed to allow me to move to Youngstown.

It wasn't until I got to Ohio that I realized how much of an impact my parent's divorce had on me. I was consumed with thoughts of my parents reuniting and getting back together. All I could think about was seeing my family back together again. My grades began to drop, and I was having a hard time adjusting to my new life. As bad as I wanted to be with my father, I was homesick, I missed my mom and my sister, but I was there, and I had to make the best of it.

My new life was vastly different than what I knew in Tennessee. The frigid weather caused me great strife. I was from a small town in Tennessee and the coldest day we knew was just below 30 degrees and snow would shut the city down. My father and I lived my with my great uncle and aunt, Bishop Ernest and Margret Simpson; they were incredibly supportive and encouraging to my father and me. As the old saints used to say, my aunt and uncle "were saved and sanctified, Holy Ghost filled to the bone." Now you would think that was a good thing, and it is, but to a young man that wants to experience some things, them being saved thwarted many of my plans.

I was a third generation Apostolic, my parents and grandparents were Apostolic. There were times when my aunt would talk with me while sitting at the kitchen table. My aunt was the person who was so intuitive that she would tell me about things I had done, that I thought were secrets and no one else knew except the person I did it with and me. I remember days when my aunt sat me down at the kitchen table and talked to me about life and then she would blow my mind and tell me something I had done that I thought nobody else knew. When I say they were saved I mean they were saved. During my stay with them, I was anointed to pick up music very quickly, so I began to play bass guitar early on. I was having the time of my life because music came so easy to me and since I had to go to church anyway, why not help by doing something I enjoy. When I was growing up we were not asked if we were going to church, we knew it wasn't an option. In our house, you went to church, or you had to find somewhere else to live.

Although I made many mistakes in my life, I wouldn't trade the teachings that I received as a child for nothing in the world. You see, it was in some of the darkest times of my life when I could reflect and remember my upbringing as a youngster, it's amazing how even when we walk away from God he never walks away from us. I can't tell you how many time I have told God "Thank you for not forsaking me as so many others had." Hebrews 13:5 is so true when it instructs us to "be content with such things as ye have, for he said I will never leave you nor forsake thee." I get chills just thinking about how God never left me so I say to you as run the race that is set before you with patience because if you get ahead of God, it could cost you your future as or it may cost you your life, it almost cost me mine. More about that later, but don't ever underestimate the people that God has placed in your life.

I had so much fun being saved at such an early age; some may say no way, or it was boring, or all we did was go to church, but I enjoyed it. However, I remember the very first choir director I ever had. She was First Lady of our church in Columbia Tn. and she was one of the people that made church fun and exciting for us as young people. I would even venture to say we had one of the most anointed youth choirs in the KY, TN council and she always pushed us to be our best. Some say growing up in the church caused them to miss out on a lot that the world had to offer, but I believe that being brought up in the church was going to be more valuable to me than I could ever imagine. By the age of 15, my father decided to remarry. She was such a sweet lady, and I loved how she spoiled me, but again I was still holding out for my parents to get back together.

I will admit that things were going well at first, but after my youngest sister Lauren was born, I could see a significant change, and it seemed as if everything I did was wrong. I can remember many nights I felt out of place and just knew things would be perfect this time. Once again, we had all the looks of a beautiful family, but behind closed doors, it was a different story. I remember times when I would hold my sister and sing to her. Sometimes these arguments would be over me, and that didn't make things any better. I wanted my dad to be happy and I know I was at the age now where I was smelling myself as the Elder folks use to say to us. I started to understand that statement once I had children of my own.

By the time I was in high school I was looking at the girls, and the girls were looking back at me. By the time I was 15 years old I was already having sex! Yes, the boy that was raised in the church was now setting aside all the principles of holiness and following what I wanted to do, my whole attitude changed when the girls were saying all the things I wanted to hear. So now when my stepmother would try to tell me something, I was sticking my chest out and acting like I was grown. So, one day she informed my father I was out of order with her or disrespecting her. So, my dad comes into my room and ask was it true what I had done, I looked at my father that day and called his wife a liar. WHOA! Why did I say that? My father took his fist and struck me so hard I slide across the floor. I found out real fast it didn't matter what was going on between them, he wasn't going to stand for me disrespecting his wife. I was not only hurt from being hit, but I think my feelings were hurt as well. I was so embarrassed that he had done this in front of her. To this day I love her, and we have a great relationship, and from time to time we get together, and she has even come to my home on several occasions, and I also love my sister Lauren so much and the unbreakable bond and relationship we share. However, on the day I got hit upside the head I was 17 years old, and I had all I was going to take living under my father's roof.

I remember the day I left home oh so well; it was after my father had dealt with me and he left the house right after. I made up my mind that today was the day I was leaving home. You know how some young people get mad at their parents and call themselves running away, well this was the real deal, I was leaving my father's home, and I would not return. It was around the second week of July and three weeks before my 18th birthday. I left walking not knowing where I was going to go, and I walked and walked until finally, I ended up in Niles, Oh. Now understand from Youngstown Oh. to Niles is about 15 miles from where we lived. I knew I had to go somewhere, so I called a brother from my church in Warren Oh, and Bishop James L Tyson was our Pastor. I called my friend and told him where I was, and he came to get me, this was a big relief because now I knew I had a place to stay for the night.

To those of you whom may feel like you have all the answers at this stage of your life, stop and take a good long hard look at yourself. Please note that you will never be able to move forward in life if you can never see anything wrong with yourself, you must be honest with yourself. At the age of 17 years old I should have been taking a long hard look at myself.

Understand when you refuse to face the truth about

who you are, then you are lying to yourself. If you

believe in not being true to you, then everything you do

in life from that point on is just trying to fix a lie. It's

when you stop trying to fix the lie, that life, and you

start to be true. How do I know this, because I put

myself in many dangerous situations all because I felt

nothing was wrong with me, something was wrong with

everybody else, nothing was ever my fault it was

everybody else's fault. At some point, you should be

real with yourself. I went through life for years blaming

everything I did on the fact that my parents got

divorced when I was younger, and it just messed me up

emotionally. One day God got my attention and said to

me "Just stop it!" Don't go through life blaming your

bad choices on your past.

I finally made it to my friend's home, still not knowing where my next move would be. I began to share with him the reason I had left my father's house, so after talking with him most of the evening, he decided to allow me to stay at his place for a while. Although I was relieved to have a place to stay, I knew my problems were beginning because of the way I left my father. Just imagine the wrath I would feel from him had he known where I was, so I decided since I was a few weeks from seeing my 18th birthday I would hide out until then. I remember my dad asking around to see where I was, but I didn't want him to find out for fear of having to answer to him. I had it in my mind and rumor had it as well that if they found out where I was, I would go to the juvenile center. This was not the place for me, so at this point, my life takes another turn, and I go into what I call survival mode.

Survival mode was new to me because I was the kid that never had to worry about anything. When I left home I left everything, all I had was the clothes on my back, that was it. I didn't know what to do, this was one of the scariest times of my entire life, but it was a decision I made so now I had to live with it. I began to understand the true meaning of the saying "You don't miss your water until your well runs dry." Don't get me wrong, I appreciated having a place to stay, it was a nice place, but now I had to take care of myself. There were many nights I thought of going back home, but see my problem was I already thought I was grown and had all the answers, so pride set in and said, "You know what you are doing, you don't need the guidance of your father, you can do this." I have often wondered what my life would have been like if I would've just settled down and listened. I knew my dad loved me and wanted the best for me, but sometimes when you are young and have a lack of maturity or none at all, you tend to follow what pride says, and you lose all sight of the direction that God was trying to take you in from the beginning.

It's a bad decision when you step out of the will of God. I began to realize real quick that I was a miserable wreck with no victory anywhere in sight. I needed God to do something for me, I wanted to feel victorious, but It seemed as if God had left me at this point, and it's at this point when I began to make some bad decisions that will affect me in the days to come. Finally, I am 18 years old, so I know it's time for me to face my dad. I go and talk with my father, and he asks me "Are you sure this is the path you want to take?" Here was my chance to come back home and what do I do, you guessed it right I said: "Yes this is the path I want to go." Here I had the chance to come back to the good life, and I listen to that voice of pride instead of my father's voice of reason. He said, "Ok, you can get your things and go." I just knew I had life all figured out, so I got my things, and once again I was walking away from my father's house, with no direction, no plan, no job, just an idea of how I thought life was going to be for me. I stayed in the Warren/Niles Ohio area for about nine months or so, and I then moved to Akron Ohio. I had the chance to meet some people there, and they offered me a place to live, and I began playing for Livingstone Apostolic. I was feeling good at this point, and it was a new place with a new beginning.

At this point, a fresh start was just what I needed. I got to Akron, and I was enjoying the fact that people were smiling and enjoying what I had to offer through my music. I was pretty good at this point, at least that's what they told me. Being a musician brought plenty of attention my way, but if you don't know how to handle the attention and remain humble, ultimately things can spiral out of control for you. Don't ever forget the gift that you have is because God gave it to you; it's not because you are so good or deserving of the gift. It's so important to know the value of what God has placed inside of you. Never get to the place in life to where you think you can be all you can be without the guidance of the Lord. There is a major difference when you ask God to help you and when you ask Him to lead you. I would soon find this out at a young age.

Just take a moment and reflect on how fast my life has gone. Between the age of 12 to 18 I had to watch my family as I knew it fall apart, my dad was gone, I had moved to Ohio, left my father's house, moved to Warren Ohio, and now living in Akron Oh. with the Scott family. That's a lot, and I hadn't made it to 20 years of age yet, but it gets even more interesting, just hang with me. So, I lived in Akron, and I had the pleasure of staying with a wonderful family. I am telling you I can't think of a better place to be at this time of my life. I became good friends with their son Gerald. We played at the church together, and Deacon and his wife were just kind saints of God and adopted me right into the family. They were wonderful people and gave me invaluable direction for my life. When I look back over my life, I thank God for all of them. Now I am having fun, I am around great people, going to a great church, and just enjoying life as best I could. I remember looking forward to going to the district meetings and the councils, and the conventions. You couldn't tell us we were not cool, this was the fun part of being saved. I got the chance to play at some of these meetings too; it was the greatest honor a young guy like me could ever ask for. We would change clothes 2 to 3 times a day, had our own hotel rooms, and try to get the attention of a young lady we wanted to talk to. So much fun, I mean we would go to church and then go to Denny's afterward and talk half the night and look forward to the next day. I truly miss those times, because the church is so different and political today. It's all about whom you know these days. Today most of the well-known preachers won't even speak or talk to you, and some musicians and singers can be the same way. However, it wasn't like that when I was on the scene, I never felt like I was so good to where I couldn't talk to people or help someone else become better at what they were trying to do.

In Akron one night in February I was asked to play at a regional meeting in Canton Oh. One of my dear friends Sis Sherry mentioned to me there was a young lady she wanted me to meet. So I went to church that night and played, still not knowing who she was because I wouldn't get the chance to meet her until after service. I met Jill after service; it was very different the way we would meet. I remember being introduced to her by the front door of the church. She smiled, and I was smiling too, so I asked her if I could call her, but neither of us had a pen. We looked down at the floor, and there was a pen. I remember the two of us laughing and saying it was the Lord's will that I call her. Shortly after that, we were together every chance we could get. It was only a 20-minute drive from Akron to Canton, so we were able to see one another a few times a week.

It was at this point in my life I realized I liked dating someone a few years older than me. Jill was 25, and I was 18, you may say why would she date someone so young, but you have to remember that by the time I was 18 I had gone through more than most 25 years old. So, we became a couple and the months are just going by. One day in September of the same year we were faced with having to go to our Pastor because we found out we were going to be parents. I was happy about this, but the hard part was facing the Pastor. It wasn't as bad as we thought it would be, that was just one of the things I loved about Pastor Byrd he was easy to talk to about anything that was going on in your life. We went into his office and told him the news, he then sat us down from anything we were doing in the church, and his next question was when do you plan on getting married? Wow! I wasn't ready for that question, but at that time in the church, if you got pregnant, the honorable and the right thing to do was to get married as long as the man had a job. We sat down and gave his question some serious thought and decided marriage

was the right choice for us to make, so in October I am

19 yrs. old, and now I am a married man.

THERE I WAS

"The way of a fool is right in his own eyes, but a wise man listens to counsel."
Proverbs 12:15

At the time of my first marriage, I was 19 years old, and my wife was 26. By now I'm living in Canton Ohio which is where she was from and started playing for a church there and later landed a job as a car salesman. Many people because they are saved now, or found God tend to forget that they had struggles at one time or another, and so did we. We went to church every Sunday and enjoyed spending time with each other. When Jill and I got married, and she was almost six months into the pregnancy, and I wanted her to meet my family in Tennessee. The marriage took place so fast I didn't get to invite most of my family. So Thanksgiving weekend we traveled to Nashville Tn., and my family embraced and welcomed her to the family.

I remember the feeling of being 19 years old and married and expecting a child, but just as I began to feel as if I was on the right path and preparing myself for this beautiful new addition, tragedy struck both of our lives, and it changed both of us in a way we could not have imagined. Forty five days into our marriage while we were in Nashville Tn. on Thanksgiving Day my wife went into early labor, and we lost our daughter. There I was, 19 years old and still learning about life, and I'm wondering what will I do now. I knew now more than ever I had to be emotional support for her. To think we left home to enjoy a wonderful holiday and instead of celebrating we are now grieving over the loss of our child. So many thoughts were going through my mind, it's only been one month after we were married and this happens. I could not understand this no matter how I tried. I knew I had to pull it together because although I was experiencing a loss, I couldn't even begin to imagine what my wife was feeling at this point.

I did all that I could to be the best support I could be, and after a while, we made it through. However, something changed about me that would take our marriage on a serious rollercoaster ride from an emotional standpoint. I began to realize how fast my life had gone and felt as if I was missing out on some things. After all, I was 19 years old, now I am not making excuses, but after the loss of our child, I began to make some terrible decisions that would cause my marriage to fail after a few years. In all that we went through, two rough pregnancies later we were blessed with our two sons, and they have brought great joy to my life. I would find out 16 years later that I already had a son by a woman in Akron and she never told me after we stopped talking that she was pregnant. Later, I would build a relationship with him after missing out on 16 years of his life. His name is Norman, and I love him and my other two sons all the same.

Allow me to share something with you, although Jill and I had sinned, we both felt like we were doing the right thing by getting married. To all of you young men out there that may be faced with a decision Allow me to share an advisory moment with you, never allow yourself to do anything that you know you're not ready for. So many times we do things for validation of others and trust me when I tell you that never works. If you are not prepared for marriage, don't mess up somebody else's life because you know you aren't where you should be. Take care of your responsibility and man up. I failed to do this, and it hurt so many people. With proper advice and me being a man it didn't have to be this way.

See I grew up in a church where if you had sinned and a child was the result then marriage was the only option. The real man will face up to his responsibility and take care of his child no matter what. Now, I am not saying that marriage is not a good thing, because it is. Most importantly God honors marriage, and He loved family so much, that he was a part of a family himself, but you have to be ready for it. If you're not, be honest and be the best father you can be and seek wise counsel as to how to be better. Jill tried for some years to give me the chance to grow up and be a man, but I wasn't ready. Unfortunately it caused so much pain, not only to her and my two son, but also to myself. My advice to all men today is to be sure you cover your wife and be the priest of the home, and a great provider and best friend to your wife. I will talk more about that later in the book.

After I got a divorce, I began to put my life back together, but it wasn't going to be easy. Instead of things getting better, it seemed as if it got worse, it was as if I existed in a big world that I knew nothing about. I felt like a failure at this point, because I had vowed that I never wanted my children to experience going through a divorce or their family falling apart. Now at the tender young age that they were, they had to grow up without their father in the home. My sons are my heart; every man loves knowing he has sons to carry on his name. Although I was young, I was determined to stay in my sons' lives. My goal was never to be divorced because I knew what the effects of going through something like this had on my life, and I never wanted my children to go through this, but it happened, and I knew I had to do my very best to be the best father I could be now more than ever.

Some days were very challenging during this time, imagine two young babies looking to see their father and he was no longer there and let's also take note my sons were 3 and four years old, but they knew I wasn't there. I would watch how this was affecting them, and at times it would break my heart. I would beat myself up so many days because I felt like a failure because my marriage had fallen apart, but I learned through this period of my life that sometimes change could bring about chaos. I didn't want to go through the change, and I wanted to see instant results.

For those of you who may be going through a time like this in your life remember that it's so important that the two parents focus on what's important first and foremost. You have to learn to establish a relationship for the sake of your children. Once Jill and I did this it made a world of difference in the lives of our children, and to this day we are what I would consider friends

and our sons have moved on into adulthood, and we

can still communicate with each other, try it, it works.

Once we tried this, I soon realized that instead of

feeling like a failure I learned that success is not to be

measured so much by the position that one has reached

in life as by the obstacles which one has overcome.

THE STRUGGLE IS REAL

"There is a way that appears to be right, but in the end
it leads to death. "
Proverbs 14:12

At the conclusion of the last chapter, I talked about the struggle and how the loss of my child caused me to realize exactly how real life is. Wow, what a blow, to lose a life at an early age just as I was learning about life itself. To be very honest I had no idea what to do or what to say; I had now experienced something that I've never thought would happen to me. Everything I learned in the church had not prepared me for this type of life event, and instead of drawing closer to God I acknowledged Him only for a moment. I had failed to entirely trust Him to get us through this life event of losing a child.

However, I knew I had to do something and that something was to Man UP. I had to help my wife at the time to get through this ordeal someway somehow. What will I say to her, how will I comfort her? We talked, and we prayed together, and life seemed to come back together like normal but something was still missing and that something was me.

Earlier I told you about not being ready for marriage at 19 years of age, and now one of the main reasons I got married was because a child was on the way. Now there is no child, and I just lost it. I lost my focus, and I was so disconnected from life as I knew it because I no longer cared. After this loss, I became someone that I didn't even know, and that's how the devil will trick and deceive you. He will make you believe that your something that you're not and I had to realize I wasn't a man at all I was a boy. Keep living, life will teach you how to Man UP and you will either Man Up or die. Please understand it doesn't matter where you go, if your mindset doesn't change you have accomplished nothing but experience and habits that are hard to be broken until there's a change in your mind.

I experienced this the hard way; it wasn't the way that I had to go, it was the path I chose. I spent so much time blaming everyone else for my mistakes; rough childhood, my parents got divorced, I left home at an early age, and none of these things were the fault of anyone. You are responsible for your decisions and your actions. The boy in me disconnected from his responsibility and from what a real man does in life and because of my decisions it almost cost me my freedom and my life.

My life between the age of 19 and 24 was tough, and now I was in survival mode. Understand at 19 years old the first job I ever had was that of a car salesman. I was only 19, but I was good at my job and at this age I was making about $4,000 a month and in 1988 that was good money. When the winters would come this was not the job you wanted to be doing; there was little to no money being made during these times. I was young and didn't have a good sense of how important it was to save money, so I was spending as soon as I made it.

After a season of doing this, I began to look for something more, but I wasn't willing to change my style of living. So I left the sales job, and for a while, I began to work different temp jobs, this was not going to last long either, it just wasn't enough money for me to do all I wanted to do. By this time, I'm 20 years old, and things aren't going quite the way I need them to go. A good friend of mine who recently transitioned this life, he says to me one day, "Hawk, we can come up and get whatever we want in life." At this point in my life I was in pure survival mode and as long as I didn't have to sell drugs I was down.

He proceeds to introduce me to his aunt we will call her Mary. I'm wondering in my mind why are we going to Aunt Mary's house. When I got there, she changed my life with the things she showed us. I knew what she was teaching me was wrong, but by this time I was so disconnected I didn't care. I just wanted her to show me how to get the money, and that's precisely what she did. Well, she got me started, and from there we got creative. So the life of crime began. I started getting credit cards that I'd never heard of before, and before I knew it, I was so deep into my lifestyle that it turned from survival to an addiction and I wasn't turning back for anything because the things, cars, money, and the women were coming too easy. Later I would figure out that it was the devil talking to me because God wasn't a part of any of the activities I was involved in. You have to be careful of the decisions you make, they can and will make or break you.

Once I learned how to do this, I realized this was easy, and I didn't have to work hard to get it, but I wanted more, so I took things to a whole different level. See instead of working like ordinary people were supposed to do my job was to wake up every day and think of how I could beat the computer and the system. At age 21 money is no longer an issue for me. I had every major credit card you could think of, and my family wore the best of the best. I drove any car I wanted, and at times I would have to decide which car I would drive. I would never have less than four vehicles at a time and all brand new, and most days I would drive one car for a part of the day and switch out to another on a few hours later. Now one would think this is a success, but it wasn't, what I had was an addiction to the lifestyle I had become accustomed to. I was so bad that when the new car smell wore off out of the car, I no longer wanted it. I could ride down the street and see a car I liked, and within a week I would have it. I thought I was so smart because all of these things were so easy for me to obtain.

Almost anywhere I would go in the city people knew me by my material things. It was nothing for me to walk up to someone and unexpectantly hand them hundreds of dollars at a time. I even had a limo service that I could call at any time, and this service would take me anywhere I wanted to go. I am sure some of my friends that read this will remember those times. I remember one time I was in Canton and I didn't want to drive to Nashville, so I called the limo and had the driver take me from Ohio to Nashville just for the weekend. As I pulled up to my mother's home and got out of the car,

I remember her taking me into her room and asking me was I in the mafia. We laugh about it now, but it wasn't funny then. I never told my parents or those close to me what I was doing, because I never wanted them to be involved in anything I was doing. Deep down inside I always believed they knew something wasn't right, not even my wife at the time knew what was going on. So I am getting money, driving beautiful cars, and of course these things were appealing to women as well, but I was more interested in acquiring material things. I thought I couldn't be touched. I was always so careful, and because of my mindset, I thought this made me successful.

I wasn't successful at all and after doing all of this I was still in church every Sunday playing for the choir. I know what God has delivered me from, which is why I don't have a problem with sharing my story with you.

This book is not about making money; it is about helping someone that's on the brink of making a bad decision that will change the entire course of their life. There are people are sitting in the church every Sunday, and they are living a double life and believe it or not they want to be delivered, but they are at a place to where the devil has them so bound up they can't even call on Jesus. They want to stop what they're doing, but church folk will judge them if they reach out. They say "I won't tell anybody, this is between me, you, and God" and as soon as you walk away your business is going over the airways. So many of us have sat in the presence of God and God was there, but you couldn't feel him.

It's so sad once we are delivered and set free we act as if we can't help our brothers and sisters. This attitude becomes a problem to others that want to be set free, and God is going to hold us, The body of Christ, responsible if we don't do something different than what we have done in the past. Due to the mistakes I made in life, I know all too well how it feels when people talk and stare at you because of what they think they know about you, truth be told most of the time they have your story all wrong or they add to it. I was doing all of these things that were wrong, and I knew God had a calling on my life, but this life I was living was more appealing and exciting than me doing what God was tugging at me to do. I knew before I had gotten too deep into this lifestyle that God wanted me to preach His Word, but I turned a deaf ear. I would soon learn that if God has a call on your life or He has predestined you to do something for Him, Trust me He will get your attention, well this is how He got my attention.

One night I was told that this kingpin in the city wanted to speak with me about business. I had nothing to hide, he's got money I've got money so what could be the problem with meeting with him? I can still remember this night so clear in my mind because this was the night I was supposed to die. He owned a small café, and I agreed to meet him there. I remember I introduced myself to him and we sat down in a back room. He started to ask me questions as to how I was able to spend money like he was and how was it that I was changing cars every 3 to 6 months and it was at that moment one of his guys put a gun to my head. His very words were "I think you're moving in my territory and I can't allow that." I'm pleading for my life and trying to explain that drugs are not what I do. Of course, he didn't believe me, and at this point, I made the decision if I'm going to die it's not going to be on my knees begging, but it will be a fight. I carried a gun as well but it was in my car, and my friend that was in the car had no idea what I was dealing with inside until he saw the back-door swing open and he jumped out of the car with the gun yelling "Let him go!" They intended to put me in the trunk, but I wasn't going. I decided to turn to try a get away from the angle of the gun, but when I did that he pulled the trigger! Guess what God did: The gun didn't go off! At this point my friend who had my gun had the upper hand, and I was released, and as I walked away I reminded the guy I came to see I don't do drugs, and I don't sell drugs. From that night on I never had another issue with the guy, and at times I feared that he would come back at me again, but he never did. Now that should have been enough to get my attention, but I hadn't learned my lesson yet.

In October of 1990 my youngest son was only a few months old and I decided to take a trip with a friend of mine to do some shopping at a mall in IL. We took a flight from Canton to a mall there, and I felt that something wasn't right before I got on the plane but I went in spite of my feeling. We got to IL, took a limo to the mall and told the driver to pick us up in 3 hours so we could catch our flight back to Canton. I went in and had purchased about $3,000 worth of clothes. As we were leaving out of the mall to get back into the car, I was face to face with law enforcement, and I'm not just speaking of the local police. Here I am thinking I was catching a flight back to Ohio and now I am sitting in a cell in IL. I was questioned about what I had just done and how could I have pulled it off, and then the biggest surprise was I had been being watched for about two years and never knew it. They had pictures and all the

evidence they needed to put me away for a long time.
In the beginning, my bond was set at $5000, I intended
to bond out and never come back to that place again,
but God had a different plan for me. He wanted some
alone time just He and I, so within 48 hours I was
indicted, and my bond went from $5,000 to $50,000
with no ten percent, now I knew I wasn't going
anywhere.

I asked myself why did I have to come here to be
arrested. The Lord spoke to me clearly and said: "I have
need of you and this is your last chance to hear my
voice, or you will die." I guess you know my response! I
hired an attorney from Ohio to come and represent me,
and when he came, the best offer that was on the table
was 25 years Federal time. Yes, the things I was into
required me to serve Federal time, this was the best
attorney money could buy, but God had a different

plan. Although I knew I heard God speak to me, I was still trying to fix the situation myself. So, after my attorney came to me with this offer I fired him and went with a public defender. After all, if he couldn't make a better deal than that, then why did I need him?

Every day I would sit in my cell, no visits from family because I was too far away and at this point, I began to understand why I was in Il and not Ohio. God didn't want anybody to reach me but Him. All I had to look forward to was making a phone call and I couldn't do that like I wanted to because of the cost. So here I am now can't do for my family, and it's looking like my kids are going to grow up without me. As I sat there I realized that all the stuff I had meant nothing now, I went back to my roots, I was praying and fasting and calling on Jesus like never before. That may sound funny but it's true, God now had me in a place where I was going to listen to what He had to say.

One morning after being in this place for 34 days it was about 2 a.m., and I said to God "If you deliver me from this I will preach your word." Now I have shared some low points of my life throughout this book, but this was the lowest I had ever been. Once I surrendered my will to God and said "It's all about what you want from me now," it was at this point that things began to shift in my life. I spent 35 more days in jail, and it was now my day in court for my sentencing. My attorney had prepared me for the worst, but I knew I had made a vow to God, and my fate was in His hands. I was the last case called that day, and they took me before the judge, and he began to talk to me about how I didn't have a criminal background and how I came from a good home. As he is saying these things I'm thinking I am going to prison, but maybe I won't go as long as my attorney said I was going for, so I am feeling scared, and I am still praying too. After he says all of this he looks at me and says "No one person should be able to pull off all the cars, loans, credit cards as you have and so I have no choice but to agree with the prosecution and sentence you to 25 years in federal prison with credit for time served."

I am standing in this courtroom ready to cry, my knees were shaking, and all I was thinking about was "Lord I promised I would do what you asked me to do, why is this happening this way?" The judge left the courtroom and went into chambers and before they took me out of the courtroom the judge came back in and instructed the officers to bring me back before him, I thought to myself "Oh my God, he is getting ready to give me more time because he forgot something."

Instead, he begins to say to me "I don't understand why I am doing this for you, but as of today you are released to go home, but if I hear of your name coming up in anything else I promise nothing will stop me from imposing this time on you." Wow! Just writing this takes me back to that day and I still get so overwhelmed with emotions when I look back at what God did for me. He gave me another chance, and I went from 25 years in prison to making a phone call to a probation officer once every six months for two years, and to top it all off I have worked for several companies since that time, and none of this is even on my record. What God was showing me and what He is trying to show you is no matter where you may be in your life right now it's not about what you have or whom you know. Whatever you may be going through right now God will deliver you but He wants the Glory, and He alone will get the Glory

when He brings you out.

HERE I AM

"A man's gift maketh room for him, and bringeth him
before great men."
Proverbs 18:16.

Before I found myself too far away from my roots, I knew that I had a call on my life not only to be a musician but to preach the gospel. Preaching was the last thing I ever wanted to do because I grew up around Pastors and Bishops right in my own family. Seeing the things they would go through from time to time just made me say "There is no way am I doing that." I told God that I will be the best musician ever if he would please let this pass from me. So, I ignored the call and went on with my life as what I would call normal.

Normal for me at age 18 was survival mode. Every day that's what my life was about, how I would survive to see the next day. However, the call wouldn't go away. I have a dear friend who had started preaching at 18, and by that time I received my call to ministry, he had already been preaching for three years. Some of you may know him, he's a friend, but he's also my current pastor Bishop C. Shawn Tyson. We would spend summers together in Ohio, and I was amazed at his music ministry, but also how God used him to bring forth His word. Mr. James had it determined in his mind that he loved playing music with his friend but you can have that preaching, and I didn't want that mantle.

I was happy and satisfied watching my friend go forth with no envy or jealousy. Although there was still something missing and me being me I decided to continue to ignore the call. Now two years had gone by, and I knew without a doubt in my mind that this is what I was supposed to do but I continued to keep that one word within the forefront of my mind, BUT! God had continued to show patience and mercy, but I took Him for granted for many reasons in my mind. Like Moses when he tried to use the excuse that he had a speech issue not to lead the children of Israel. Eventually, he soon got over it and accepted the call and was one of the greatest leaders in history. Deep down inside that's what I wanted, was to be great in God but just not through preaching, lol anything but that, just let me be great in another way.

Now three years had gone by, and I finally get up enough nerves to go to my then pastor and tell him that I had been called to ministry. He says "All right I want you to be faithful and sit a while and learn." I'm wondering to myself what is that supposed to mean "sit and learn"? Back then just because you went to the pastor and said you were called to preach you didn't just get up the following month and preach your first sermon. You had to make full proof of your ministry, and your leader knew when you were ready. You had to be faithful to everything going on at church and outside of the church. Nowadays we have gotten away from those principles, but that's another subject for another day. After talking to the pastor and I began to wait and wait...then I waited some more until I decided I'm not going through all of this for him to choose when I can go forth, I'll keep on doing what I've been doing, and everything will work out. I felt I had done my part by telling my pastor I had been called, but he wasn't moving fast enough for me. I was tired of waiting, so I stepped back into my comfort zone, big, bad mistake.

One of my favorite books in the bible is the Book of Proverbs and the reason why is because of the wisdom and simplicity of the book. Proverbs allow you to live, breath, and understand practical principles as it relates to our everyday lives. Although this book is one of my favorites, it's not as easy as it seems to live up to. I was at a place in my life at one point where I felt useless, worthless and good for nothing. Have you ever been at a point in your life where you felt as if you were trying your hardest and it seemed as if nobody was paying attention? Maybe that's not your testimony, but it was indeed mine. After my wilderness experience, I realized just what God had done for me. You may ask just what did He do for you, well I'm glad you asked. In the simplest of terms, He saved my Life. Every day you wake up is another day you have an opportunity to do something great. The key word here is YOU. I had to stop looking at people to open the door for me. The truth of the matter is Most people don't care about your story. Most of you may not agree with that statement, but I can only speak from my personal experience. I've had people listen to my story and act as if they cared and did nothing but tell my business. I had to live with the regrets of even sharing my story because I was indicted for speaking truth thinking I was helping somebody and thinking this may open a door for me. The fact is, telling your business isn't always the best way to go.

Allow me to share how my gift has made room for me and continued to make room for me. One was my intentions. The intention of what's in your heart will show in the life that you live. Some people are around me and are in contact with me right in my local church and they don't know the intentions of my heart. I've often wondered why is this. The problem is most people are so connected to clichés, and you don't fit in, so they never get to experience the real you. Please, whatever you do, focus on pleasing God and live life for yourself and stop living it through and for others. We can lose so much time by not tapping into what God truly wants for us, but remember there's a gift inside of you.

So I had to ask what proves my heart? The Lord spoke to me and said, "Stop looking for people to validate you. I am the one who will open the door." Now I have heard this statement over and over again down through the years, but it didn't register until I had to apply it to my own life. It's funny to me now some of the things that I was doing was just to be accepted by other people. I was doing everything from giving money to buying dinner for 15 to 20 people at a time, and I thought to myself that people would approve of me and see that I genuinely had changed. In truth all they did was spend my money, get a free meal, and later I would still hear about the whispers of people saying "Yeah, that was nice but watch out for him." I'm crying out to God saying "Lord I did nice things for the Bishop or the Pastor or the members or even my family members and yet nothing has changed." My prayer was "Lord why has thou forsaken me?" I had to refer to Proverbs 18:16, the scripture says "A man's gift maketh room for him, and bringeth him before great men." I was trying to present myself, and all the time God was waiting for me to step out of the way. When I stepped out of the way, my gift, that God-given gift, began to make room for me. I know some of you may think that I had to do something, and yes you are correct, and I'll get to that in just a moment. However, when I moved God moved, if you don't remember anything else in this entire chapter, please remember this and say it to yourself, "When I move God will move."

Now I have had the distinct honor to sit among great men. I've had the opportunity to preach in places I thought I would never go. Also, some of the doors that God opened for me were opened by people who at one time or another thought I wouldn't make it or quite fit the mold, reputation, or status quo they were looking for. However, when I moved God moved, and all I had to do was walk in with humility and humbleness of heart.

A lot of times in the various circles we run in we are told to jump up and down, run around the church ten times, or even give a certain amount of money, and God is going to turn your situation around in 24 hours. Now let me put this disclaimer out here, I'm not saying that in many cases God didn't tell the preacher or the pastor at that time to say those things, but I also know that after the reaction you must now take action. We must always remember as human beings our make-up is that we are emotional people. You may not always show your emotions all the time, but deep down inside you are an emotional being. So, a lot of the things we react to in most cases are out of emotion because of

our need or our present circumstance or situation.
However, when you are looking for the gift that's in you
to make room or to bring you before great men you
have to in turn and spring forth into action. After all of
the jumping, shouting, speaking in tongues, and many
of the other theatrics we do, God requires an effort for
the door to open.

What I will say to you is that if you want the gift
given to you by God to make room for you and bring
you before great men and have a feeling of self-worth
without seeking validation from men, you have to
believe in who you are regardless of what anyone else
thinks or feels. My advice for you and the action that's
going to get you there, as it did for me, will be to LIVE
the message that you speak about. Your life is a living
sermon, and the actions that you display are a
testimony. I've heard a lot of sermons, and I have

preached a lot of sermons, but the best ones are the ones that people can witness because of the life that you live. So, you have to do as I did, stop looking at the people around you and live your best life on a daily basis. Your gift will be seen and magnified in places you never imagined. People's lives will be changed just by watching the sermon that you show them on a daily basis before they ever step foot in the church.

Throughout this book, I've shared with you some of the darkest places in my life as well as well as some of the high points. However, through all of it, God has sustained me and kept me. For those of you that read this book and you may be in a dark place, God will do the same for you. Society will attempt to make you believe that once you messed up, you are doomed for the rest of your life and this thought process simply put is just not true. As you read my story you have to understand, as I had to learn, that life is what you decide, and it does not have to be what others try to dictate it to be. When I was facing 25 years in prison, I felt like my life was over and many others did as well. They counted me out and even went as far as to say I would never be much of anything. The most hurtful part was the indictment that came from the church, it came from Pastors, it came from Bishops. I'm not quite sure when this strong desire to fight came about in my life, but it did, and when it happened, I was more determined than ever that I was going to come back. I must admit at first it was to prove a point to all those that doubted me, but then I had to realize how important it was for me to focus on how far I had come and not how far I still had to go as it related to taking my life back. Whatever you are trying to achieve in life

PRESS every day toward your goals and it will happen right before your eyes.

Had I not pressed to regain my place in life and believed what the naysayers said about me, I would've turned away from God and the church. However, there was such a determination to make a comeback, I refused to give up. Yes, I have reaped many times over because of my actions. Some of the stories aren't in this book, and I'm not a perfect person today but one thing I know for sure is that regardless of where you may try and place me or what your opinion may be of me, I'm not the man I once was. I can only write this to you today because of God's Validation, NOT validation of man.

Proverbs 3: 3-4 reminds us that when we hold tight to love and faithfulness, we will "win favor and a good name in the sight of God and man." God will handle it all. There are many pastors, bishops and even laity as a whole that will spend their lives and all of their efforts and energy to please man. However I say to you at this very moment, "Please God, and life will happen like you never thought it would." Yes, I was a people pleaser at one point too because I believed that was the way back, but I soon realized the only way back was through God himself.

We need to get to that place where we realize that if our mess is put on public display, where would we be? How would you feel after trying your best to get your life back only to become subject to a Spiritual Indictment? In the body of Christ, there is no room for this at all. I'm sure many may disagree with my stance concerning indictments but if people can't come into our churches and our homes and feel love then what are we doing all that we do for? Not only should we show the love of Christ to those outside but inside as well. The judgments and Indictments need to stop even among our brothers and sisters that we see weekly and daily. Measure your place in life not as how others view you, but how God sees you and fight every day of your life to be the best you that you can be. A businessman once said, "Don't compare your beginning to someone else's middle." If you're not careful, mentality this comparison can take you to a place you don't want to go. Life is not a competition. Just think about how flowers grow, from the time the seed is planted in the ground it grows at its own pace, grow at your own pace and when you develop this strategy in life, life is less stressful and more enjoyable because this is the way God intended for us to live.

I wish that I could tell all within this one book but it's impossible to do, but I will say this, "the BEST for me is still yet to come" and I see it more and more each day. Reprogram your mindset and Fight.

ABOUT THE AUTHOR

Pastor James Hawkins resides in the Midwest and has been in ministry as a Senior Pastor and currently serves as an Executive Pastor.

He has had the distinct honor to travel across the country as a preacher, teacher, and musician. He is a husband and proud father of 3 sons one daughter and 2 Godchildren and proud Grandfather of 10. He is also the founder and owner of JHM Radio which is one of the fastest growing radio stations in the entire Midwest.

91637673R00051

Made in the USA
San Bernardino, CA
31 October 2018